CRYSTAL

MY FIRST PERIOD

SKYLAR MCBRIDE

Copyright © 2024 McBride Collection of Stories

All rights reserved.

ISBN : 9798302740809

TABLE OF CONTENTS

Central Park Adventure ~~~~~~~~~~~~~~~~~~~~~~~~~~~~ 5

Crystal's Confusion ~~~~~~~~~~~~~~~~~~~~~~~~~~~~~~ 6

Ebony Explains ~~~~~~~~~~~~~~~~~~~~~~~~~~~~~~~~~~ 9

Learning Together ~~~~~~~~~~~~~~~~~~~~~~~~~~~~~~~ 10

Introducing Pads ~~~~~~~~~~~~~~~~~~~~~~~~~~~~~~~~ 13

Lunchtime Bonding ~~~~~~~~~~~~~~~~~~~~~~~~~~~~~~~ 17

Gym Class Confidence ~~~~~~~~~~~~~~~~~~~~~~~~~~~~ 18

Options Discussion ~~~~~~~~~~~~~~~~~~~~~~~~~~~~~~ 21

Understanding PMS ~~~~~~~~~~~~~~~~~~~~~~~~~~~~~~~ 22

Packing the Kit ~~~~~~~~~~~~~~~~~~~~~~~~~~~~~~~~~ 25

Shared Experiences ~~~~~~~~~~~~~~~~~~~~~~~~~~~~~~ 26

Crystal's Reflection ~~~~~~~~~~~~~~~~~~~~~~~~~~~~ 29

Crystal's Tips for Dealing with Your First Period ~~~~~~~~ 31

Crystal's Friends Share Their Tips! ~~~~~~~~~~~~~~~~~ 35

Tips for Parents: Supporting Your Child Through
Their First Period ~~~~~~~~~~~~~~~~~~~~~~~~~~~~~~ 37

Glossary ~~~~~~~~~~~~~~~~~~~~~~~~~~~~~~~~~~~~~~~ 40

CENTRAL PARK ADVENTURE

Crystal loved living in New York City. The tall buildings, busy streets, and bright lights made every day feel like an adventure. But it was the weekends she looked forward to most, when she and her older sister, Ebony, would spend the day together. They explored the city, tried new foods, and visited unique shops. Each outing was like a new chapter in a never-ending book of experiences.

"Where do you think we should go today?" Crystal asked, her eyes sparkling with excitement as she tugged on Ebony's arm.

Ebony grinned, her eyes lighting up. "How about we head to Central Park? We can grab some street food and people-watch. I heard there's a new art show by the lake!"

As they strolled into the park, the sun shining above them, Crystal could feel her heart swell with joy. The air was filled with the sounds of music from a nearby street performer and the laughter of children playing. Central Park, with its green lawns and trees, was always a place that made Crystal feel at home.

CRYSTAL'S CONFUSION

One morning, Crystal woke up feeling strange. She looked down and saw bloodstains on her sheets. Her heart raced as confusion and panic flooded her. "What's happening?" she thought, her mind spinning. She sat up in bed, staring at the unfamiliar sight. Was she hurt? Was it serious? She quickly stood up and rushed to the bathroom. The sight in the mirror only intensified her worry.

Her stomach tightened, and she felt a knot of panic rising in her chest. She needed answers, but who could she turn to? Her mom was at work, and the last thing Crystal wanted to do was freak her out. Then, she remembered Ebony.

With her mind made up, Crystal ran to her sister's room, knocking frantically on the door. "Ebony, I think something's wrong!" she exclaimed, trembling. Ebony, who had been sitting on her bed reading, looked up with surprise but quickly set the book aside. She stood up, walking over to Crystal and pulling her into a warm hug. "It's okay, Crystal. You just started your period," she explained, gently rubbing her back. Crystal felt a wave of relief mixed with confusion. "A period?" she whispered.

EBONY EXPLAINS

"What's a period?" Crystal asked, her voice small but full of curiosity. Ebony, always the patient and wise older sister, smiled gently and sat down beside her. "A period is when your body sheds the lining of your uterus. It's completely natural and happens to all girls as they grow up. Your body's just doing its thing," she explained calmly.

Crystal's wide eyes reflected a mix of wonder and worry as she processed the information. "Does it hurt?" she asked, her voice trembling slightly. She had heard stories from her friends, but she wasn't sure what to believe.

Ebony nodded slightly. "It can sometimes be uncomfortable, like cramps in your belly, but there are ways to manage it. Don't worry, I'll teach you everything you need to know." Crystal smiled, grateful for her sister's reassuring words.

Just then, Ebony's voice softened. "You're growing up, Crystal. And that's something to be proud of."

Crystal nodded slowly, still a bit confused but feeling comforted by her sister's calm explanation.

LEARNING TOGETHER

"Why do people have periods?" Crystal asked, her brow furrowing slightly in thought. Ebony smiled, grateful for her sister's inquisitiveness. "It's part of your body's preparation for having kids one day, although that's way in the future!" she added quickly, seeing the puzzled look on Crystal's face. "Your uterus builds up a lining every month, and if you don't get pregnant, your body sheds it. It's your body's way of making sure it's ready."

Crystal tilted her head thoughtfully. "So, it's like my body is getting ready, just in case?" she asked, piecing it together. Ebony grinned, proud of how quickly her sister was picking things up. "Exactly! And don't worry, it becomes a routine over time. You won't even think about it after a while."

Crystal smiled slowly, feeling reassured. "I guess that makes sense. It's kind of like my body is preparing for something big."

Ebony nodded, "Exactly! And there's no rush. You've got plenty of time to learn about your body.

INTRODUCING PADS

Crystal stood in the feminine care aisle of the neighborhood drug store, her eyes scanning the shelves packed with colorful boxes. There were so many options—pads, tampons, liners, and even things she'd never heard of. Her stomach fluttered with nervous energy.

"Ebony, how do I even choose?" Crystal whispered, glancing around to make sure no one was listening. The aisle felt too quiet, making her self-conscious.

Ebony placed a reassuring hand on her shoulder and smiled. "Relax, Crystal. Let's start simple." She picked up a package of regular pads with wings and handed it to her. "These are great for beginners. They're comfortable, and the wings help keep them in place."

Crystal examined the package, reading the bold words on the front. "Ultra-thin? That sounds… less scary."

"Exactly," Ebony said with a wink. "They're super easy to use. You just have to remember to change them every few hours—around 4 to 8, depending on your flow."

Crystal nodded but hesitated. "What about all these other ones?" She gestured to the tampons and menstrual cups.

Ebony laughed gently. "Those are options too, but let's take it one step at a time. Pads are the easiest to get started with. Once you're comfortable, we can talk about the rest."

Crystal sighed in relief. She liked having Ebony by her side, guiding her through this new and slightly overwhelming world. "Okay, pads it is."

As they made their way to the checkout, Ebony leaned down and whispered, "You're doing great, sis. I'm proud of you."

Crystal smiled, holding the package a little tighter. For the first time all day, she felt a spark of confidence. "Thanks, Ebony. I think I've got this."

Ebony grinned. "I know you do."

That morning, Crystal woke up feeling proud. The trip to the drug store with Ebony had been more than just picking up supplies—it had been a step toward feeling confident and prepared. She carefully packed her new pouch of essentials into her backpack, giving herself a little pep talk in the mirror before heading out the door.

By the time she reached school, Crystal felt ready to tackle the day. But when Ms. Lopez announced that their health and wellness project presentations would begin after lunch, her stomach flipped.

"Crystal, you're up first," Ms. Lopez said with an encouraging smile.

As the afternoon wore on, Crystal rehearsed silently at her desk, reminding herself of everything Ebony had told her. She could do this. By the time the bell signaled the start of health class, she felt a mix of nerves and determination. Clutching her colorful poster, she walked to the front of the room, ready to share what she had learned.

LUNCHTIME BONDING

At lunch, Crystal sat nervously with her best friend Maya. She had just shared with her that she had started her period, and it felt strange to talk about it out loud. "Welcome to the club!" Maya said, giving Crystal a warm hug. "Don't worry—we've all been there!"

Crystal let out a relieved sigh. It was nice to know she wasn't alone in this. Maya reached into her bag and pulled out a small kit. "Always carry supplies in your bag," she advised, holding up a pad and a small packet of wipes. "Trust me, you never know when you'll need them!"

Crystal smiled, feeling more supported than ever. "Thanks, Maya. I feel much better now," she said, her confidence growing as she realized her friend had her back.

GYM CLASS CONFIDENCE

Crystal hesitated before gym class. She was worried about how she would feel during physical activity. "What if I get cramps?" she asked nervously, adjusting her gym clothes.

Maya, ever the sarcastic one, shrugged casually. "What's the worst that could happen? It's just cramps. You walk it off or you complain about it until they stop."

Sofia, on the other hand, offered a more optimistic perspective. "Don't worry, Crystal," she said cheerfully. "It might feel uncomfortable at first, but listen to your body. Take a break if you need to and hydrate! You've got this!"

Crystal took a deep breath and nodded. "Thanks, guys. I think I'll give it a try." Maya handed her a water bottle with a wink. "Hydration is key. You'll feel better, trust me."

As they entered the gym, Crystal felt a little lighter. She wasn't sure if she could run a full lap just yet, but with her friends' encouragement, she was willing to give it a shot.

OPTIONS DISCUSSION

Walking home from school, Crystal couldn't help but wonder about other options. "What about tampons?" she asked, turning to Ebony. "Are they better for sports or swimming?"

Ebony smiled and nodded, holding up a box of tampons. "They're great for sports and swimming," she explained. "You'll get the hang of it when you're ready. But remember, there's no rush."

Crystal smiled, relieved. "It's good to know I have options," she said, feeling more in control of her body and choices.

Ebony grinned. "That's the key—finding what works best for you!"

Crystal nodded, feeling supported by her big sister. "Thanks, Ebony. I'll think about it."

UNDERSTANDING PMS

"What's PMS?" Crystal asked as she and Ebony sat in the kitchen, sipping tea. The cozy warmth of the tea and Ebony's calm presence helped Crystal feel at ease.

"PMS stands for premenstrual syndrome," Ebony explained. "It's what some girls experience before their period. Things like mood swings, bloating, or even headaches."

Crystal furrowed her brow. "So it's like my body giving me a heads-up that my period is coming?"

Ebony nodded, taking a sip of her tea. "Exactly. It doesn't happen to everyone, but if it does, there are ways to manage it. Exercise, eating well, and even relaxing with a heating pad can help."

Crystal smiled, her tea warming her hands. "That's good to know. So it's like my body's way of sending me signals?"

"Exactly," Ebony said with a grin. "And paying attention to those signals can help you feel more in control."

PACKING THE KIT

With Ebony's help, Crystal packed her first period kit. Ebony laid out the essentials: pads, tampons, wipes, and a small pouch for everything. "This will keep you prepared no matter where you are," Ebony said, her voice full of encouragement.

Crystal zipped the pouch proudly, holding it up with a smile. "Thanks, Ebony. I feel ready for anything now."

"You've got this, Crystal," Ebony said, wrapping an arm around her sister. "And remember, it's okay to ask questions. I'll always be here for you."

Crystal looked at her kit again, feeling a newfound confidence. This was one more step toward understanding her body, and she was ready for it.

SHARED EXPERIENCES

At lunch the next day, Crystal sat with her friends, Maya and Sofia. She decided to share what she had learned with them. "I started my period," she said, her voice steady. "It wasn't as scary as I thought it would be, thanks to Ebony."

Maya smirked and leaned back in her chair. "Well, welcome to the club, Crystal. Mother Nature's special gift to us all."

Crystal laughed, grateful for Maya's humor. "It feels good to know I'm not alone in this," she said.

Sofia smiled warmly. "You're not alone at all. We all go through it, and you're doing great! I like to think of it as a superpower—it's proof that we're strong and amazing."

Crystal grinned, feeling the support from both sides. "Thanks, guys. It really means a lot."

CRYSTAL'S REFLECTION

That night, Crystal sat by her window, looking out at the glittering city lights. The soft hum of New York City buzzed below, but the calm night sky above captured her attention.

Her diary was open in her lap, and she began to write. "Dear Diary, today I learned so much about myself. Growing up is a little scary, but it's also exciting. I feel stronger knowing that I can handle it."

She paused, tapping her pen against the page as she smiled to herself. "I have an amazing sister and incredible friends who've helped me so much. I feel like I'm ready for whatever comes next."

Crystal closed her diary and hugged it to her chest. The stars outside seemed to twinkle just for her, and she felt a peaceful sense of pride. She was growing up, and she was ready.

CRYSTAL'S TIPS FOR DEALING WITH YOUR FIRST PERIOD

DON'T BE AFRAID – IT'S NATURAL!

Starting your period is part of growing up. Every girl experiences it, and it's a natural process. It's nothing to be ashamed of, so take a deep breath and embrace it!

BE PREPARED

Carry a small period kit with pads, tampons, wipes, and an extra pair of underwear in your backpack or purse. You never know when you might need it, and being prepared will help you feel confident!

TRACK YOUR CYCLE

Use a calendar or an app to keep track of when your period starts. It'll help you predict when it might come again, so you can be prepared ahead of time.

STAY HYDRATED

Drink lots of water! It helps prevent bloating and keeps your body feeling good during your period.

REST AND RELAX

Periods can come with cramps or fatigue. Taking naps and using a heating pad on your stomach can help ease the discomfort.

TALK ABOUT IT

Talking to a trusted family member, like your mom, big sister, or aunt, can help you feel less nervous. Don't be afraid to ask questions or share how you're feeling.

TREAT YOURSELF TO COMFORT

When you're on your period, it's okay to pamper yourself. Take a bubble bath, enjoy some chocolate, and watch your favorite shows. Self-care is important!

YOU'RE NOT ALONE

It may feel weird at first, but remember, every girl goes through it. Talking to your friends can make you feel less alone, and they may even share their tips!

YOU ARE STRONG

Even when it feels uncomfortable or overwhelming, remember that you are strong. Your body is doing something incredible, and you're learning to take care of it!

CRYSTAL'S FRIENDS SHARE THEIR TIPS!

Here's what Crystal's friends have to say about navigating your first period. Together, they've got you covered with honest advice, practical tips, and a whole lot of love!

MAYA'S TIP
"Always keep an emergency kit in your bag! Mine has a pad, an extra pair of underwear, and a small pack of wipes. You never know when you might need it!"

SOFIA'S TIP
"If you're feeling moody or crampy, try some light stretches or deep breaths. And don't feel bad for taking a little break when you need it!"

JADA'S TIP
"Don't be afraid to talk to someone if you're confused or feeling weird. My mom and big sister helped me so much. And now we're here for you too!"

AMARA'S TIP
"Get to know your cycle by tracking it. I use an app, but you can also write it down. It helps me stay prepared and understand my body better."

TIPS FOR PARENTS: SUPPORTING YOUR CHILD THROUGH THEIR FIRST PERIOD

CREATE A SAFE SPACE FOR QUESTIONS

Encourage open conversations about periods. Let your child know it's okay to ask questions and share their feelings without judgment or embarrassment.

NORMALIZE THE CONVERSATION

Talk about menstruation as a natural and healthy part of growing up. Share your own experiences (if appropriate) to help them feel less alone.

PREPARE TOGETHER

Help your child create a period kit with essentials like pads, wipes, and a change of underwear. This small step can make them feel more confident and prepared.

EDUCATE ABOUT OPTIONS

Explain the variety of menstrual products available (pads, tampons, menstrual cups, etc.). Start simple and revisit the topic as they grow more comfortable.

TEACH CYCLE TRACKING

Show them how to track their cycle using a calendar or app. It helps them anticipate their period and understand their body's patterns.

BE PATIENT WITH EMOTIONS

Hormonal changes can cause mood swings or heightened emotions. Offer patience and understanding, reminding them that these feelings are normal.

PROVIDE RESOURCES

Share age-appropriate books, videos, or websites about menstruation. Giving them access to information can empower them to learn at their own pace.

CELEBRATE THIS MILESTONE

Acknowledge their first period as a positive step toward growing up. A simple treat or special activity can help make this transition feel less daunting.

BE PREPARED YOURSELF

Familiarize yourself with common period-related challenges (e.g., cramps, PMS) and solutions. Having remedies like heating pads or pain relief available can be helpful.

ENCOURAGE A SUPPORTIVE NETWORK

If they feel comfortable, encourage conversations with trusted siblings, family members, or friends. Knowing they have a network of support can be reassuring.

GLOSSARY

- ☆ **Menstruation**: The monthly process where the lining of the uterus sheds if there's no pregnancy, often called a period.

- ☆ **Puberty**: The stage of growing up when your body changes and becomes more like an adult's body.

- ☆ **Cycle**: The time from the first day of one period to the first day of the next. It usually lasts about 28 days but can vary.

- ☆ **Hormones**: Chemicals in your body that help control how you grow and develop.

- ☆ **Pads**: Soft absorbent materials worn in underwear to catch menstrual blood.

- ☆ **Tampons**: Small tubes made of cotton inserted into the body to absorb menstrual blood.

- ☆ **Cramps**: Pain or discomfort in the lower stomach, common during menstruation.

- ☆ **Ovulation**: When an egg is released from the ovary during the menstrual cycle.

- ☆ **Sanitary Products**: Items like pads, tampons, and menstrual cups used to manage periods.

- ☆ **Hygiene**: Keeping your body clean, especially during your period, to stay healthy.

SKYLAR MCBRIDE

Skylar McBride is an accomplished 11th-grade honor roll student, author, and event organizer from Queens, NY. A student at Brooklyn College Academy, she balances her academic achievements with her passion for storytelling and leadership. Skylar is also a proud member of her high school's step team, showcasing her dedication to teamwork and discipline.

Since beginning her writing journey in February 2020, Skylar has authored and published four captivating books. Her works span various topics, including children's fiction and cooking, reflecting her creativity and versatility as a writer. Skylar's books aim to inspire and entertain young readers while fostering a love for reading and learning.

Beyond writing, Skylar has organized successful book release events and signings, where she managed logistics, collaborated with vendors, and designed promotional campaigns. Her innovative approach to event planning and marketing has helped her books reach a wider audience.

Skylar's passion for storytelling, strong work ethic, and commitment to inspiring others make her a standout voice in young literature.

VISIT
www.mcbridestories.com

 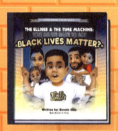  

 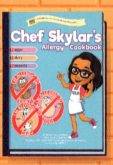 

Printed in Great Britain
by Amazon